Public School Gatekeepers

The Customer Service-Driven School Office Professional

By
Kelly E. Middleton

Edited by
Mike Mavilia Rochester

Public School Gatekeepers: The Customer Service–Driven School Office Professional

Published by Kelly E. Middleton
30 W. 8th Street
Newport, KY 41071
www.kellymiddleton.com

Edited by Mike Mavilia Rochester
Layout by Sophie Hanks
Cover Design by Arash Jahani

ISBN: 978-1-7374608-0-0 (paperback)
ISBN: 978-1-7374608-1-7 (ebook)
Library of Congress Control Number: 2021916641

Whatever you are, be a good one.
—Abraham Lincoln

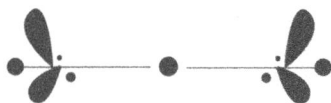

This book was written in collaboration with a few outstanding school office professionals I've worked with over the years.

This book is dedicated to the memory of Connie Reffett (February 14, 1953–January 6, 2021).

Contents

Preface

Public School Gatekeepers is my fifth book about customer service in public education. It is the third in my series of books geared specifically to a particular department within the school. The others are *Simply the Best* (teachers) and *Feed Our Students Well* (food service).

Over my thirty-plus years in public education, I've realized that customer service training for office staff is severely lacking. There's no handbook for how to do this work in a way that puts the customer—students, their families, and the community—first. That's why I wrote this book: to speak directly to office staff members. These frontline workers are the face of the school and work tirelessly each day as the gatekeepers of public education.

I strongly believe that without front office staff who are trained in the concepts of customer service, a school cannot thrive. I've witnessed so many inspirational stories and practices from the office professionals in my schools, I just had to write it all down in this quick-reference guide that can be picked up and opened to any page to get a simple, easy tip on how to add some customer service flair to any interaction with guests.

Introduction

I realized the importance of customer service early in my school administration career. As a principal, I worked diligently with my main office staff and administrative assistants to ensure we made good first impressions when anyone called or entered our school, modeling how successful companies like Disney and Southwest practice customer service. It did not take long for others to notice a difference when they called or entered our school, and I began receiving requests to train and educate other school leaders and their staff in the area of customer service.

Trainings were based on what the best frontline personnel in the business world do each day to help make their companies successful. One of my favorite activities for school office staff trainings was a survey with questions about their job. In order to make these anonymous, the survey attendees were to wad up their completed surveys and throw them across the room and then pick up a waded-up survey that was not their own. One particular question has always stuck out in my mind and pushed me to write this book.

The question was, "Has your school system ever given you training on basic customer service principles?" Participants would then look at their paper to see how someone else in the room answered the question. I then asked those with a paper that had answered "Yes" to go stand on one side of the room and those with "No" answers to stand on the other side of the room. I have done hundreds of these trainings and it's rare to have anyone stand on the "Yes" side. Each time, when they all got to their places and looked at how the room had divided up, they would inevitably break out in laughter. Then I would say, "And we wonder why the public has such a negative perception of our public schools," and I would see the light bulbs go on in their heads.

The reality is, most school office staff do not get training on these aspects of their jobs. But they should. Many school leaders simply do not know how to train employees for customer service, but that's no excuse. Can you imagine Disney not properly training their frontline employees? What about Chick-fil-A cashiers or Ruth's Chris Steak House servers? The best companies train for customer service and, from my experience, so do the best schools. That's why this book is so important. As a public-school administrative assistant or office staff person, have you received specific training in customer service techniques? This book shows you exactly how to cool down an angry parent, which calls to put through to leaders, what to do when the phone rings and a customer comes in at the same time, or what to do if a relative comes in saying they are picking up a student but they're not on the approved list.

For the purposes of this book, when I say, "school office professional," I'm talking about main office staff and central office administrative assistants. That is, those frontline employees who answer phones, schedule appointments, greet guests, and so on. They can work either in the front office or in an administrator's office. These positions are sometimes referred to as front office clerk, receptionist, secretary, administrative assistant, front desk worker, customer service representative, clerical aide, front office coordinator, office assistant . . . the list goes on. I will use some of these terms interchangeably throughout the book.

As you know, school office professionals are at the center of just about everything happening at the school. Wearing many hats is certainly a job requirement. You are the gatekeeper of your school! You're in charge of greeting, answering phones, photocopying, dealing with administrators and teachers, and forwarding incoming messages to proper personnel (like a school switchboard). You serve as office manager, psychologist for staff who've had bad day, right-hand person of leaders, and on-the-fly nurse. In some districts, office professionals are still in charge of dispensing student medication! There are not enough pages in this book to list all the hats you wear. You are on the front lines of your school, dealing with visitors all day long, and you're often the first (and only) person at the school with whom guests will have contact. This is why it is crucial that school office professionals have exceptional customer service skills. How someone feels about your entire school can come down to one interaction with an employee on the front lines. *In my opinion, anyone who interacts with a school office professional should have a better impression of the school than when they came in or called in.* That's the goal. In order to reach that goal, you'll need to master the art of dealing with the customers.

When I was starting out as a school administrator, I quickly realized that our office professionals did so much work but received little training on how to do it correctly. I thought, if we could train them in customer service principles, we could greatly improve the quality of interactions with students, families, guests, and other school employees. I view the school office professional like an extension of the school leader; someone who can work together with administrators to solve problems and keep the school running smoothly. They've been *the* most important factors for the successes I've had in my career. We go to battle every day and I need the right people in the foxhole with me as part of the leadership team.

But it's not only for the sake of leaders that we need quality, well-trained administrative staff. School choice is more widespread nowadays than ever. Most public schools are competing for kids with charter schools, private schools, and even homeschooling. Customer service is how schools differentiate themselves from the competition and thus win over students and parents who have choices in educational options. Bad experiences and interactions with public school staff can make them turn to our competitors.

Since school office professionals have their hands in so many details of school life and have so many interactions with students, families, and the community, it's imperative that they give great customer service.

We know that giving great customer service has a huge, lasting impact on customers, whether it's first impressions or lifelong supporters. Have you ever stopped buying from a store because of a bad experience? As consumers, we will base our judgment of an organization on one interaction with one employee. With hundreds of phone calls coming into the school each day and almost as many office walk-ins, it is nearly impossible for a school to have a positive public perception with poorly trained employees in their front offices. So, if we can harness the power the school office professional has over so many facets of school operations and strive to have positive interactions with visitors, we can greatly improve the public perception of a school district. These tips and examples from my thirty-two years of public-school experience are the road map to doing so.

This book is divided into topics like how to recover well when mistakes are made, how to be exact with information, how to improve phone communication and nonverbal communication, and how to be a public relations professional to create *positive* gossip at the school. Each topic includes my tips, relevant quotes, and stories from my experience. The tips here are practices office professionals at my school have used, and they've been proven to work. They helped our schools better serve our students and, in turn, improved the public's perception of our schools.

Giving exceptional customer service can help you experience higher job satisfaction and ensure that you are made *indispensable* to the school and your leaders. I've found that so much of the school's energy comes from the office staff. Whether you put out positive or negative energy, the entire school feeds off of it. As the saying goes, with great power comes great responsibility. Are you ready to answer the challenge and ball up your survey to send a colleague over to the "Yes" side of the room?

Before We Start

This book is designed to be a quick reference guide—
something you can pick up and open to any page to learn
a nugget of information about giving great customer service. If
you already practice some of these tips, congratulations! You're
already on your way to being *the* all-star go-to office professional
at your school. If, on the other hand, you're worried you don't have
time to incorporate these tips, don't worry. You won't be able to
do all of these at once. Start with a few and go from there. I've
found that those who choose a few topics to work on are able
to work more efficiently because they are preventing problems
before they start, freeing up more time to add more of these tips
to their routine, creating a snowball effect. Take your time and
enjoy the knowledge that you're improving each day, month, and
year. I recommend having a conversation with your leader to be
clear about the limits of your role and how much authority and
autonomy you have to creatively solve problems as you see fit.

These tips aren't just about solving problems in the moment—
they will also make your job easier in the future. Every time you wow
a customer with great service, you create a new fan of your school.
Turning a neutral or even a negative opinion into a positive one will
help you next time this customer comes to you with a problem (and
you know they will be back!). When someone is a fan of you and
your school, they will be more understanding, more patient, and
more likely to assume you'll do a great job instead of assuming you
don't care or won't be able to fix their issue.

1. Be a Public Relations Professional

1. Create "positive gossip" about your school by using social media platforms such as Facebook, Twitter, Instagram, and Snapchat or use QR Codes. School leaders love when staff take the initiative to spread the school's good news, photos, and triumphs. It paints the school in a favorable light and motivates the community to follow our accounts.

I have found that the majority of a school's best and worst public relations comes from its internal staff. As a school building leader and district leader, I was frequently blessed with office professionals who knew the benefits of sharing positive news from our schools and districts, which in turn endeared their leaders to the public. Very rarely will the community believe good things are happening within a school or the school system if they do not believe in the principal and/or superintendent.

2. Use your unique skills to find creative ways to enhance the enjoyment of the main office guests. I had one administrative assistant who created a yearbook each year of our school's photos, newspaper articles, positive notes, and announcements for people to look through when they were waiting in the main office. Work with your school leader to determine other ways to improve the atmosphere within the school office. After all, people will be able to tell if those within the office truly enjoy their jobs.

3. Keep an attractive bulletin board of information for staff, parents, and students to read. It may contain advisory minutes, clubs, and open positions. It can brag on staff, students, or the school as a whole and include a calendar of upcoming events at the school. It's a one-stop spot for information for anyone affiliated with the school.

4. Working with your school principal or superintendent, put together a "key communicator list" of email addresses and phone numbers for school and/or district leadership. This list should include site-based council members, school board members, all school administrators, and people in the community who are supportive of the school district, such as alumni, former school board members, mayors, commissioners, chamber of commerce members, religious leaders, or spouses. This list can be used to disseminate important information, especially when inaccurate news comes out about the school or when negative rumors spread. It will allow them to tell the community the *real story* or the *truth* behind the story. Note: this should be a fluid list, updated as people change positions, retire, or move on.

2. Phone Communication

1. Answer the phone with a smile in your voice. "A man without a smiling face must not open a shop." —Chinese Proverb

2. Tell everyone your name. "Welcome to Acme Middle School, this is Amy. How can I help you?" During the conversation, check for ways to connect with the caller. It's much easier to inadvertently be mean to someone we do not know. Also, if the call drops or gets cut off, they have your name so they can call back and ask for you to resume the conversation.

3. Be a good listener. John Wayne once told someone he was "short on ears and long on mouth."[iii] That may have worked for a cowboy in the Old West, but as a school office professional, you always need to be listening. Is the customer angry? What is at the heart of their problem? Not talking over people and making sure you get their point are important aspects of being a good listener. Paraphrase or repeat back to them to make sure you heard correctly.

4. Answer the phone within two to three rings, always. I've witnessed staff waiting for someone else to answer the phone. This is a no-no! Remember, there's someone on the other line who has an important issue. Answering the phone as quickly as possible shows you care about their call. Letting it ring on and on (or hoping someone else answers) shows the caller you don't care about them or gives an impression of an office in chaos. Keep in mind, if there are other visitors in the office, they'll see you ignoring the phone call, giving the impression that you really do not care about callers.

5. Record a pleasant voicemail message with soft music. Consider having a recording that gives school updates and news for when people are on hold. If you can, offer an estimated wait time or the option for you to call them back.

6. Time is very important to people, so we need to be the "guardians of people's time." My late friend Janie (a member of our school board) had terminal cancer and was given a short time to live. Knowing this, she became acutely aware of her time and she had no patience for unnecessary waiting. Once, we were in line at a grocery store and the checkout person was going too slowly. Janie just put her groceries down and said, "I'll come back later."

   a. Avoid leaving someone on hold for more than thirty seconds. If you must keep them on hold longer, reconnect and give the caller an update. Nobody wants to feel like they've been forgotten about (which we all know happens). If the issue will take several minutes or even hours, give them your name again and tell them you will personally call them back. Thus, you are owning the situation. I would recommend you set a reminder to make sure this call is made.

   b. Think of ways to make procedures more functional: speed up lines, streamline processes, and make sure you aren't wasting any customer's time. This cuts down on frustration and gives people a positive opinion of your school. Discuss with leaders about making exceptions to routine situations. For example, does your school have enough ticket takers for events? If the temperature is extremely cold or there is a bad storm, can lines be moved into the school?

c. Are forms easy to read? Are there redundant questions? If the parent has several kids at the school, do they need to fill forms out for each one?

d. If an event time changes, like a sports game, make sure parents get that information! Change the time on the school's webpage, put the alert on social media, get kids to call their parents to let them know.

e. If you find that parents are always asking for directions to sports fields or off-site buildings, type up directions and have them available instead of having to repeatedly take time out of your day to provide them.

7. Be conscious of your tone of voice. Verbal communication often gets misinterpreted because the speaker's tone doesn't match the information they're giving. For most people, their response to information (good or bad) given in a rude or disconnected voice is negative.

> "We've collected the most common service complaints, and every one of them is rooted in lack of respect for the customer." —Leonard Berry, Director, Texas A&M University Center for Retailing Studies[iv]

8. Get back to people within twenty-four hours. You may have to look something up or ask someone for an answer and then get back to the caller. You want to call back as quickly as possible, so consider twenty-four hours the *deadline*, not the goal. The best companies almost always beat this call-back deadline. This is especially important for office personnel who answer calls or manage schedules for the superintendent, principal, or other school leaders. If you answer a call from a parent and leave a message for a teacher, you may need to remind the teacher to make that call back. A paper trail is always a good idea (like sending an email or writing a message on a board) so no one can say you never told them.

Customer Service Stat: 41% of consumers expect an e-mail response within six hours. Only 36% of retailers responded that quickly. —Forrester Research Inc. 2008[v]

9. Own the transfer. Have you ever called a company and were told you were being transferred, then either the call dropped completely, the phone just kept ringing, the voicemail was full, or you left a message and never got a call back? It's incredibly frustrating and makes me cringe every time I hear "I'm going to transfer you." That split second after hearing that can be panic inducing if you don't trust that these issues will be avoided. When speaking with a customer you're about to transfer, maybe add, "They always get back to people within twenty-four hours and if they don't call you back, you call me at [your direct extension] or send me an email at [your email address], and I'll make sure they return your call." By doing this, you will address the customer's fear that they are just being passed off and that their issue will not get resolved. I'd add that you should be careful about transferring a call without knowing for sure the person is in the office or if they will answer the call. When I call companies, I always wonder if the person will even listen to their voicemail. Making sure all callers' issues you pass off to others get resolved is truly giving great customer service.

10. Role-play and/or record yourself on the phone. Ask others to listen or practice with you. Ask people like your immediate supervisor for tips. I hate doing this myself so if you've got the courage, there's nothing better than hearing how you sound when you talk to people. Certain tones, inflections, and even emotions come out in our voices without us realizing it. This can be an invaluable tool to improving your phone-speaking voice and helping you improve your customer service tone.

In an August 2015 survey of 1,016 US adults regarding the most irritating customer service pain points, not being able to get a live person on the phone and speaking to a rude or condescending person on the phone tied for the top spot. Think about that. Not getting a live person on the phone is equally irritating as having a rude or condescending person helping you.[vi]

From this same study, the top seven most irritating customer service pain points were:

1. Can't get a live person on the phone
2. Customer service is rude or condescending
3. Disconnected
4. Disconnected and unable to reach the same rep again
5. Transferred to a rep who cannot help
6. No customer service phone number provided
7. Long wait on hold

"Memorable customer service can only take place in a human-to-human situation." —Jeffrey Gitomer, Author and Professional Speaker[vii]

3. Be a Professional

1. Dress professionally. I've found that when staff dressed down, the students didn't respond as well to them. This happens in every aspect of life: a sloppy appearance does not command respect. If you have trouble with what to wear, maybe have a friend help you make a Pinterest board with great office looks. Self-confidence in the way we look projects an attitude of pride and professionalism and can make your job easier. Also, consider purchasing school gear to show your school spirit. If you don't want to shell out the money, you could volunteer to work at an event and ask for a shirt or hat as your reward. I've found that staff working out deals with coaches, theater directors, and the music department has been a great way to get more people involved and to wear our school gear.

2. Act professionally and do not let people see you sweat under pressure. The best school office professionals don't get frustrated and lose their cool. They may be sweating on the inside, but they don't let it show. As you know, people feed off our tension, so keeping your cool can diffuse a situation or keep it from escalating. We all know the main office is a hub of drama in the school: dealing with students who got in fights, parents frantic that they can't find their children, staff mad at each other or you because the copy machine broke—the list

25

goes on. So, it takes a lot of effort to keep that tension down. If you've ever had a waitress, store manager, or customer service person on the phone lose their temper with you, you know how quickly it can turn you off to the organization or at the very least create tension in the moment.

3. Make sure the office area looks professional and welcoming. Robert Moore, the Chief of Schools for the Jefferson County Public School District in Louisville, KY, says, "Keep workspaces neat and organized. Visitors will be in and out daily. A neat and organized space gives the appearance of a safe and orderly environment." Seating, walls, and floors should all coordinate. Create a color scheme. Everything on the walls should be level. Furniture should be in good condition. You don't have to spend a lot of money, but they should look neat, clean, and professional. Inject some school pride by hanging school banners, the mission statement, or any awards on the walls. One of my pet peeves is a messy office. I find it distracting and so will some of your guests. Another pet peeve of mine is spelling mistakes on signs. What message does it send that the adults at a school don't even know how to spell? When in doubt, look it up and have someone else read it. Let's look great and be grammatically correct.

Tips from My School Office Professionals

Q: If a staff member came up to you and said they were just hired to be the assistant to the superintendent and they wanted some advice on how to do a good job, what things would you tell them?

A: Be a good listener—make sure you know exactly what your leader needs in order to be successful. Be able to change direction mid-project. Juggling several projects at one time is crucial to being a good assistant. —Susan Hensley, Administrative Assistant to the Superintendent at Mason County School District

A: One of my former bosses told me to always make him look good. I have always been loyal to my boss and have their back because you don't always know the whole situation. I've found, in most cases, decisions are made in the best interest of the student and/or teacher. Always trust your boss. —Kelly Grayson, School Office Professional at Straub Elementary School in Mason County and former Assistant to the Special Education Director, Newport Independent Schools

A: You are the face of the top office in the district. Wear it like a new dress and shoes. Listen! You will find out many things that will be helpful to know. Be ready for anything to happen. Stay calm in the worst situations. Be ready to wear many hats and be happy that you've been given the opportunity to serve. —Kim Klosterman, Administrative Assistant to the Superintendent, Newport Independent Schools

4. Help keep backstage issues backstage. Keep unhappy people and discipline out of the main office. Parents, students, and the community are always coming in and out of the main office, so it needs to be free of drama like arguing teachers, sick students, or students who have been fighting. When you hear any negative gossip about the school or staff, make sure you let leadership know so they can be informed and possibly stop rumors from spreading. As a superintendent, I love for office staff to listen and "report the whispers before they become screams." In other words, reporting problems before they're out of hand! This idea also includes making sure the school social media pages and the webpage are free of internal drama. Monitoring our online presence is crucial to the job and will ensure your school isn't airing its dirty laundry for the whole community to see.

5. Maintain a positive attitude and never take complaints or angry statements personally. Being on the front lines, it's important to remember that customers' problems are almost never personal. You could even play a game with yourself by seeing how long it takes you to diffuse their anger or solve the problem. Take pride in those tough situations where you can turn around an angry visitor and make them a school or district supporter.

6. Maintain confidentiality at all times. Often, my top office professionals have had to copy information for me that was confidential or open my mail for me, so there is a lot of trust necessary in this relationship. In addition to protecting the privacy of leaders, you may need to do so with students' medication and medical records, teachers or staff who may have pay docked for child support, staff who may be getting divorced, or other legal issues. School office professionals must be the "guardians of information," making sure to protect the privacy of students and staff. Maintaining confidentiality will go a long way toward showing your coworkers, bosses, and students that you care about their privacy, making you a more trustworthy employee.

7. Admit when you make a mistake. Parents and guardians do not expect you to be perfect; we all make mistakes and there are so many issues coming at you all the time. This job is not for someone who needs to be perfect. Arguing about who is at fault just wastes time. The quicker you admit a mistake, the more accepting people are of the error. Being defensive or waiting to apologize tends to cause people to have a stronger negative reaction than an immediate admission. Own it so we can move on to the next important issue.

8. Learn how to recover when you make a mistake. Research from J.D. Power and Associates shows that recovering well from a mistake can actually be *better* than not making a mistake at all because it shows humility and honesty.[viii] Customer service expert Ken Blanchard says that in order to recover well, "an apology should be immediate, sincere and equal to the offense."[ix] For example, a primary school student kept missing the bus because a substitute teacher wasn't getting the students out on time. It got to the point where the parents were calling and (rightly!) complaining about this issue. One of my front office staff came to me and told me the situation, asking if there was any way we could drive the student home so the parents didn't have to drive to the school another time to pick up their student. I ended up driving that student home myself, and the parent was won over by the gesture of the busy principal taking time out of his day to personally make sure the student got home. Of course, I apologized profusely to the parent and made sure this problem got fixed. By recovering well from mistakes like these, you'll be able to win over new supporters of your school.

9. Help staff and students recover well when they make mistakes. Once you become experienced with this skill, help others by being the calming force to support them. This will make you a valuable resource to everyone. Teaching staff and students about the art of recovering well boosts school morale and creates a positive school culture.

10. Be sure to always give customers your full attention while you are helping them. I know it's a slow day if you're not doing ten things at the same time. But when a customer comes in, you'll need to drop the other nine. If you are working on something else while a customer is talking, like organizing files, some form of paperwork, or answering an email, the customer is going to presume they do not have your full attention . . . and they're probably right. Making eye contact shows that you are engaged with just that person. Remember, customers expect that you will not be distracted with any other work or people while you are helping them. So, if you don't do that, you're not meeting their minimum expectation. If there's some unavoidable interruption, make sure you first acknowledge that you're being pulled away and give an empathetic apology. Be sure not to give that issue too much time before you get back to the original customer and either pass them to someone else or pass the interrupting issue to someone else.

11. Double-check information with the customer. I mention this in the section on Phone Communication but want to reiterate here. Take notes when with customers and read back all the information to make sure you have everything correct. Pay particular attention to phone numbers and email addresses. But it's much more than making sure we get numbers and emails correct; it's truly letting the customer know that we listened to them and we care.

4. Be Exact with Information

1. Tell customers the reasons behind decisions or policies. Sometimes it helps people accept an answer they don't like if they understand the rationale behind it. For example, a sign reading, "Doors are shut to keep in air-conditioning," or a memo to parents or on social media reading, "School dismissed early because weather reports show a storm will be coming at noon. For the safety of students, we feel we need to end early today." Nobody likes hearing "because that's our policy" as an answer to their problem. Find a way to give more clarity on the decision. If you can't, it may be time to sit down with your leadership to understand the rule. Maybe the rule needs to be changed or tweaked.

2. Know your flag etiquette. Who lowers the flag when needed, takes it down in the rain, replaces it when tattered, and so on? I suggest you take time to learn all the caveats because there are always people in every community, especially veterans, who will call if Old Glory isn't treated with proper respect.

3. Make sure the marquee has current information and, when dates of events pass, change them immediately. People will drive by that marquee twenty times, never internalizing what it says . . . until it's outdated. For some reason, people tend to notice those mistakes and they are a glaring sign that we aren't on top of things!

4. Keep a notepad and make notes when people call or come into the office. Keep these pads and even store them for future meetings. There is just too much going on in a school office to expect the brain to remember every detail! You may be surprised how handy keeping these notes may be when that issue comes up again or if a leader later on asks when it happened or what transpired. Having these notes will be your backup if anything goes wrong.

Product survey company End User Feedback says that 27% of email inquiries are answered incorrectly. That's too high! Knowledge of the product is more important than speed when emailing a customer, so do everything in your power to get it right the first time, every time. Public schools cannot afford to be wrong one in four times they send an email to parents.[x]

5. After hearing visitors, students, or staff relay an issue, sum up the conversation and recap the end goal. Remind them what you are going to do for them, what they can expect to happen, when it will occur, and how to get back in touch with you if it does not happen as planned. If there is a next step, state who is doing it and by what date. When speaking with a parent, relay the message and the timeline to respond to the appropriate staff member. For example, when relaying the message to a teacher, say, "I told Ms. Johnson that you'd get back to her by Tuesday."

5. Be an Office Manager

1. Think ahead and anticipate customers' needs in all areas of the school or district. Remember, you are the gatekeeper! Solving problems on the fly isn't the best strategy. Taking the time to think through and be a step ahead of the chaos will save you time and reduce stress. For example, have a box of tissues on hand when bad news is being given. For Grandparents' Day, have you thought about the dietary needs of this older crowd? The food you serve to students may not work for them. If it's an elementary school, are you going to make grandparents sit in the little chairs at those little tables? Many may have hip, knee, or balance problems. What will you do if it's a rainy or stormy day and the visitors need assistance getting into the school? I like to say, if you are not planning for service, you are planning to fail.

2. Show initiative. The best office professionals present ideas and think critically about procedures and rules. At one of my prior schools, parents had to write notes for kids to change buses or for a kid to miss a school day. Some didn't write well or had trouble with spelling. So, one of our administrative assistants made prewritten forms for some of the most common notes parents would need to write for students. Another initiative was part of Move-Up Day. Our office professionals posted a list in the window of the school with

each student's teacher assignments and a list of supplies they needed for the start of the school year, making it easy for the parents to see this important information at a glance. One of our front office staff had the idea to reach out to the local school supply store to communicate the teachers' lists to them. Parents could just walk into the store, go to the school supply section, and find a display for each teacher's class with all the necessary supplies.

3. Thoroughly inspect spelling and grammar. There are people in every community that love to catch organizations making spelling mistakes and post them online. I am convinced they live for it! Help your school and leadership by proofreading everything you make and be on the lookout for mistakes on signage others have made. Regularly check the walls, marquees, and notices. This goes especially for anything the school puts out to the public like social media posts, press releases, or anything on the school's website.

Chief Proofreader

I remember a graduation night as superintendent where the high school principal had misspelled a school board member's name in the program and left out the prefix "Dr." on another member. TThat night, after the excellent graduation ceremony, I had two board members questioning our school principal's attention to detail. Another time, I had a different principal honor a school board member with a coffee mug with the district logo and the board member's name on it for school board appreciation month. The only problem is that the company had misspelled the board member's name. If gifts are personalized, someone needs to check the gift's spelling before it is wrapped.

The above typos our staff missed do not do justice to the countless errors they *caught* while proofreading materials we produced over the years. In fact, I could fill another book with all the errors we've found! As a former teacher, principal, and superintendent in multiple schools and districts, one constant I found was that there was a very high bar for perfect grammar and spelling on anything coming from or posted inside a school or district.

In 2016, Donald Trump was elected president of the United States and was our first president to use Twitter to reach millions of followers (approximately 89 million at the time of this writing). Many times, there were multiple spelling and grammar mistakes within the same tweet. I was embarrassed and could not help thinking, "He is the president . . . could he not have someone proofread his tweets?"

4. Celebrate important holidays with staff, students, and parents. Work with your leader to create holiday-themed events, decorations, menus, and so on. Some examples our office professionals have coordinated include: Fall Festival, Italian Festival, White Elephant party/Secret Santa/Yankee Swap with staff, opening-day breakfast, and teacher appreciation day. Your school should have an appreciation day for every department each year, as these days are recognized on state and national levels. (A comprehensive list of important dates by calendar year is provided in my book *Competing for Kids.*) Organizing these events should include buying gifts for staff appreciation days, cooking or delegating who's cooking for potlucks or celebrations, buying cards and making sure they get circulated throughout the staff, putting up decorations for each holiday students and staff may celebrate, and organizing events for homecoming/founders' days or whatever traditions and special days are important for your school.

5. Make sure the office always smells good by using plug-ins, flowers, or air freshener sprays. Consider using seasonally scented plug-ins. We all know that walking into a pleasant-smelling room creates a great first impression. It may even calm down an angry visitor. There will always be someone who hates a particular smell and loves to complain about anything that's new; it is our job not to let these people ruin it for everyone else. Make sure the office gets cleaned thoroughly each day to prevent odors from building up.

6. Help leaders to make sure restrooms are stocked appropriately for guests, students, and staff. Remind custodial staff to prepare restrooms for high traffic days like Grandparents' Day and Parent Teacher Conference Night. This tip reflects the attitude of "owning the school." Making sure the appropriate personnel know about important days will ensure they do a thorough job and that your visitors have a pleasant experience.

7. Learn how to fix the copy machines and other equipment for teachers. I've known office professionals who were master mechanics when it came to copiers, vending machines, and pencil sharpeners. Be the MacGyver of your school. This will help relieve the stress teachers experience from broken copiers, contributing to a better school environment.

8. For repairs that you can't do yourself, keep a list of emergency phone numbers. For example, if the copy machine went down, and teachers are panicked, who is the person that can come fix the machine immediately? Or let's say someone just flushed an entire roll of toilet paper down the toilet in the boys' bathroom and water is going everywhere. Who is the custodian or maintenance person to call? What are the options if this happens after school during an athletic event? Who's the backup person to call in case this one is unavailable? When speaking with repair companies, try to get the cell number of a service technician. Having emergency numbers readily available will allow you to take the burden off your leaders and be the reliable go-to person at your school when repair emergencies occur.

9. Have a plan for when a teacher or any staff person gets sick during the school day and has to leave. Consider keeping a list of emergency substitutes on hand so you can quickly find a fill-in at a moment's notice.

As a school principal, I could usually find substitutes when teachers called in sick. While the quality of instruction the students received might not be the same, the day would still be salvageable. However, the days when my top office staff were absent were insane. Many times, I just wanted to go home myself. In an episode of the television show *A.P. Bio,* the principal takes over the duties in the main office while the receptionist is off for a day. As you can predict, the whole school falls apart, including pine cones getting mixed up with the meatballs served at lunch and a student getting sent home with the wrong parent.[xi]

10. Put together a staff handbook with commonly asked questions. Staff will appreciate that you're doing this for them, but, really, it's going to help you the most by making sure they don't keep coming to you with questions or problems. In the handbook, include anything they might come to the office to ask you about, such as teachers' extra-duty assignments, lunchtimes, schedules and school calendars, payday, diagrams of the building, laws and fire drill instructions, purchase forms and the process for filling them out, absentee forms and how to use them, how to collect money for picture day or selling candy, and the process for requesting a personal day.

6. Relationships with Students

1. As much as possible, call every person by name and be sure to get their name correct. Some names may be very hard to pronounce so have a way of making a note for yourself and others. Perhaps write down a phonetic spelling of their name.

2. Don't be afraid of using nicknames. I love to give students nicknames as long as they are okay with it. I admit we must be careful, but it makes a nice connection with them. Some adults you know may also appreciate it.

3. Care about students' lives outside of school. Always be on the lookout for students' impactful life events when speaking with community members and reading local newspapers. Maybe they are sick, injured, or have a death in the family. If a student is absent for three days, find out why they've been out. Once you find out the reason (say they had a house fire and had been displaced), report the information to school leadership, buy a card, get a sympathy gift, or take any appropriate action. The best office professionals will be one step ahead and purchase sympathy cards, thank-you cards, or get-well cards in advance for their leaders to have on hand to fill out immediately to get them delivered in a timely manner.

4. Remind students about school events. We all know how often kids forget with their busy schedules, so helping them out in this way is a simple means to show you care. You may want to also help your school leader with reminders using emails, bulletins, intercoms, One Call systems, or when passing them in the hallway.

5. Enjoy your job and be energetic and enthusiastic. It shows! In my research, when asked, students were able to correctly identify the teachers and staff who didn't even want to be there. Students are much more aware than we give them credit for. There's no fooling the kids; we project our emotions more than we think.

6. Be an advocate to students and take up for them when necessary. From problems with home life to getting to school late and missing breakfast, students need a place to turn when they have problems. As the face of the school, you hold the responsibility to help students get the help they need. Whether it is finding the right person to help them or fixing the problem on your own, having the backs of students in need is a top priority to give great customer service.

I had placed two students in in-school suspension because they left their classroom without permission and went into another classroom. It seemed like an open-and-shut case to me. Well, later that day, one of my front office staff, Ruth, came to me and said I'd been a little too hard on them. She went on to say I should go check out their assigned classroom.

Now, I didn't follow her logic, but I trusted she wasn't trying to waste my time. When I got to the classroom, there was a substitute teacher who'd been there for several days. It was immediately clear this teacher did not have things under control. The classroom was in chaos. I then looked in on the classroom the two students had gone to after leaving their classroom. The teacher was in charge and there was actually learning going on. No wonder these students left! I couldn't blame them.

I immediately walked to the ISS room, apologized to the students, rescinded the punishment, and got to work fixing the classroom management problem. I made sure to thank Ruth for leading me to the truth.

Good things happen for kids when everyone not only knows and buys into the mission, but also has the confidence and the ear of the leader to help them succeed at their position. I was thankful that Ruth and I had a close enough relationship that she felt comfortable pointing out a problem that contradicted my actions. I see this closeness as an asset, and a good leader will as well.

7. Don't let students slip through the cracks. Build relationships with students you see that could use extra guidance and support from an adult. Be on the lookout for students who may get in trouble at school or who lack social skills and friends. Connecting and sharing a joke every now and then can brighten their days and build their self-esteem.

> **Donna Says: "Some of us in the front office took it upon ourselves to take on the challenge of finding students who may be falling through the cracks or have a challenging home life. We made contacts with these students, got to know them, and mentored them. I befriended an autistic child who started stopping by my window in sixth grade. For Christmas, he gave me a book from the library's free bookshelf. He checked to see if I still had it many times afterwards. Expect to cross paths with former students often. They will remember you as a constant part of their school experience. Some relationships with students will last a lifetime. I have a student who still wishes me a happy birthday. She was one of my mentoring students."**
> **—Donna Williams, School Office Professional at Harrison County Middle School**

8. See students perform in school events beyond the school day. For example, attend plays, sports games, debates, science fairs, or any club activity. It's important to interact with students and parents while you're there. Tell them they did a good job (either right there or the next day at school), let them talk about their work, and show enthusiasm for their accomplishments. Attending events is an example of what separates those who see their job as simply a paycheck from those who see themselves as part of a community. Being the latter will propel you toward "indispensable" status. If you're practicing some or most of the tips in this book, you'll be truly indispensable to your school, making you the last person to go when cutbacks occur.

9. Show no favoritism. When calling in kids to help in the office (office helpers), or letting kids do announcements, be sure to rotate students who do those jobs. Parents may ask to change bus assignments and you may be tempted to oblige because you know them. That can come off as favoritism, especially if/when other parents find out. With staff, if you do something special for one person, word will get out so make sure you're willing or able to do it for others. Avoid cliques and getting roped into helping your friends over other staff. This concept is all about perception. Be sure you aren't perceived as playing favorites. The best way to do that is to be consistent in how you respond to parents, students, and staff.

10. Dress up for Halloween and other holidays. It's okay to have fun with students and be silly. Maybe put out a candy bowl with themed treats or baked goods. I've found that students really appreciate when the adults at the school get excited about holidays and create a fun, celebratory environment. Excitement and happiness are infectious, so you can really boost the mood at your school. You might even end up enjoying your job more!

> **As a former public-school student, I remember a lot more about how I was treated by the staff at my schools than anything I was ever taught by any individual. As a parent, I remember how I was treated in the office when I called or stopped by more than why I ever called or visited in the first place.**

7. Relationships with Staff

1. Speak to any staff person you see when you're walking down hallways or sitting at your desk. Always say hello and goodbye (bonus points if you can say it in another language). This tip is a good one to use with any person, including students, parents, and community members you see.

> **"Attention is the rarest and purist form of generosity."**
> **—Simone Weil, 1909–1943, French Essayist and Philosopher[xii]**

2. Find ways to remember staff names or look them up in advance of an upcoming meeting. Call them Mr. or Ms. unless you know them very well or they ask you to use a less formal name. Everyone likes when someone knows their name.

3. When a staff person is sick or has to miss school because of a major issue in their personal lives, help your principal and other school leaders with sympathy cards, phone calls, and visitations. Find out what room they're in, visitation times, and any other pertinent information. If a staff person or their close relative passes away, get details for funeral services, directions, and any pertinent information. Write a memo to staff or inform your administrator and schedule their time accordingly.

4. Offer your personal time to staff members (within reason). Help decorate a room or space for an event; cook or bake for staff on occasion. Consider volunteering to take tickets at a game or event or watching a teacher's kids in the main office while the teacher works late after school. Keep a box of coloring books and toys on hand for such occasions. There are endless ways to give time to staff.

> **Kim Says: "One year, I volunteered to help with the school musical. I overheard the drama teacher talking about how they were struggling with costumes and makeup. I love fashion and makeup, so I was excited to share my knowledge to help out my school. I helped students backstage at each rehearsal and all the performances. While it was a big time commitment, I often reflect fondly on those long nights spent with our wonderful students. Some of the students even came in to see me for years afterward, sharing their latest roles in the upcoming plays."**
> **– Kim Klosterman, Administrative Assistant to the Superintendent at Newport Independent Schools**

5. Have a secret candy stash for staff. Sometimes a piece of chocolate can make a bad day turn around for all of us. Making your desk a little oasis for staff who need a five-minute break and a few M&M's will endear you to your coworkers and can also make you feel good about cheering someone up with such a simple, kind gesture.

6. Understand health insurance to be able to help staff with their insurance plans. Enrolling each year is a headache for staff, so having the knowledge when they inevitably come to you with questions will be very helpful to them and allows them to stay focused on doing their job. This applies for any type of paperwork staff may have to fill out, like direct deposit forms, change of address forms, and beneficiary changes for life insurance. While it could fall into the category of "this is not my job," the more you can help a struggling teacher, the more the teacher can just focus on their students. Thus, you are positively impacting student learning.

7. Be a leader to other classified workers. Because you're so close to the school leaders, they'll be depending on you to lead by example. At many schools, the rest of the staff follow the lead of the front office staff. If the school is trying to get employees to wear their name badges, having you and the rest of the front office staff follow protocol will rub off on the rest of staff. A current example, wearing masks during school, is another case where office professionals can lead the way. If there is a volunteer list that no one has signed up for, be the first to put your name down. Leadership is contagious. Infect your coworkers with your gung-ho spirit.

8. Be a resource to the new front office professionals. Always be on the lookout for opportunities to mentor someone. Not only does it make you feel good about yourself, but it also makes them more likely to help you out in the future. Who doesn't want someone to be there when they need something? People tend to act the way others acted toward them when they started, so if your coworkers are cold or not helpful to you when you're new, you're likely to do the same toward new employees later. On the other hand, if staff are welcoming, helpful, and genuinely trying to make your transition easier, there's a good chance you'll do the same down the road. The bottom line: the better your coworkers do their jobs, the more your department will benefit.

9. Help the school leader recognize employees when they are in the local paper or receive an award or when an employee's child is recognized for an achievement by doing things like getting thank-you cards or congratulations cards. I had an office professional who would laminate articles on card stock and leave them in employee mailboxes. Consider taking a picture of them with the award and putting it on the school Facebook page. Not only does this make the employee feel good about peer recognition, but it also paints your school in a positive light to your Facebook followers.

United We Stand . . . Divided We Fall

Have you ever been to a restaurant where two employees were not getting along? How did it affect your dining experience? I remember one particular school office where the administrative assistants were not getting along with each other. Normally, if one was busy, the other would always answer the phone. If neither had someone directly in front of them, upon ringing, one of them would just pick up the phone immediately. I had a known goal of wanting the phone answered within three rings. During this particular time of the rift between the two, it was as if they were keeping track of who answered the last call. Sometimes neither had a person in front of them and they both let the phone ring three times, at which point they both would then try to answer simultaneously. I also had staff members picking up on the "chill" within the office. This was an "ah-ha" moment for me that the school office is truly a glass house. I let this small rift go on for a few days before having a conversation with these two talented ladies. I was a little nervous about this conversation but, it turns out, they had already worked it through. We had a good laugh about it and there was never another issue.

Don't think no one notices situations like this. Other staff and leadership pick up on tensions between employees, creating an uncomfortable atmosphere in the office, and it can even spread negativity throughout the school.

8. Relationships with Administrators and Board Members

1. Be on the same page with leadership. School and district leadership change quite frequently. Each time there is a new leader and/or a new office professional it's like a new marriage. Time must be carved out where both the school leader and office professional can get to know each other and discuss expectations. Guessing what is expected between these individuals in the middle of a school or district crisis can be disastrous for everyone.

2. Screen calls for your immediate supervisor. Do not let minor issues waste your immediate supervisor's precious time. Avoid routing calls to your supervisor when you can answer the question yourself. Sit down with your supervisor and create a list of who to put through and who not to put through, then update that list as needed.

- Which calls do I put through immediately? Family members? Important friends? School board? Superintendent? Important projects? Current vendors? Seasoned school office professionals know that many vendors will act like longtime friends of school leaders so you will be sure to put the call through for them.

- Who do the supervisors not want to talk with during a school day? Cold sales calls? Parents with simple questions you can answer? Come up with strategies to persuade them to tell you their question, such as, "Perhaps I can help you right now and save you some time?" You can really endear yourself to your leader by having your goal to be to put as few calls through to them as possible. You may need to have a good poker face when you have your leader complaining about the person in one ear and needing to be professional with the caller in the other ear.

3. Make your bosses look good. Brag on your school, your department, or your boss with their boss, school board, and parents. There are countless opportunities to do this. Injecting a little positivity in discussions helps. So, when the school board comes in, you can tell them things are going great at the school and share some positive news. If a parent calls while your principal or superintendent is observing a class, instead of simply saying, "She's unavailable at the moment. Can I have her call you back?" you can say, "She's busy observing a class now, but I'll have her call you back later this afternoon." Bragging on someone when they're doing something wonderful, even when it's not necessary, is a great way to make your school and fellow employees look good. These little things matter for the overall impression of your school and keeps your school competitive within today's educational environment.

Robert Says: "Having a great administrative assistant will make you shine on days you are not on top of your game. It is like having a consistent role player that you know is going to guard on every play and rebound like crazy! Dependable."
– Robert J. Moore, Chief of Schools, Jefferson, KY (and former basketball coach)

4. Keep your ear to the ground and always give your leaders a heads-up about potential issues. Working in the front office, you hear a lot: news from the community, employees talking. Leaders will always appreciate getting the heads-up that you're hearing people talking about an issue that may require attention from them. For example, during the Black Lives Matter protests in the summer of 2020, a few football players held a thin blue line flag (a symbol of police support) during the national anthem before their game. This did not go over well! Many fans were disappointed with the timing, thinking it was a statement being made by the school. People ended up boycotting the games, and the whole town was in an uproar. I believe that this was not only a planned move by a few students, but one that many people at the school had heard about beforehand. By not taking the issue to leadership, this plan was allowed to catch leadership off-guard.

> "A typical business only hears from 4% of unsatisfied customers, thus, it does not hear from 96% of unsatisfied customers. Research says that 91% will not return."
> "It takes 12 positive experiences to make up for one unresolved negative experience." "Leader's Guide: Secrets to Keeping Our Customers Happy!" by Ruby Newell-Legner[xiii]

5. Be able to work beyond the normal workday. Give a little bit extra. The best office professionals I've known have always been willing to help with school events at night or before school. A few examples are school board meetings, site council meetings, fundraising events like Halloween festivals, musical concerts, end-of-the-year activities, and so on. For those office staff who went above and beyond, I made sure they got time off when they needed it.

6. For staff who work closely with administrators, remind leaders about important meetings and school or community events that may not be on their radar. Maybe set up alarms on their phones or call them ten minutes before a meeting starts if you see them still in their office. Also, remind leaders about events happening in the lives of others close to the leader.

Below are two scenarios where my assistant and I had a great relationship and one cautionary story about leaders who won't work together with office professionals.

I believe the school and district office professionals are the most important people in determining the future success of school leaders. As principal, I had one assistant who would always ask me if I was sure whenever I asked her to do something that she thought might get me into trouble with my superintendent or someone at the district office. This additional questioning would give me some time to reflect. Sometimes, I would reconsider my email or at least tone it down to an appropriate or proportionate response.

When I was superintendent in another district, my administrative assistant was a little less forward. When she thought I needed to rethink a message I wanted to send, she would pretend she was too busy to send it for me that day. Mind you, these were the only occasions when she would ever leave work without completing a task for me. Many times, I would tell her I had changed my mind the next day . . . as she knew I might. Eventually, I figured out she was playing this little game and had my best interests in mind. I called her out on this behavior about a month before I retired, and she laughed so hard as she stated that, sometimes, she just could not get to all of my work . . . especially on days when I had written angry letters or emails.

In my time, I have seen many administrative assistants who were community leaders, who were the go-to people at the school and even running the school or district during a transition of school leaders. Then, the leader comes in and doesn't utilize the connections and strengths of this assistant. They have even gone so far as to create enemies of administrative assistants simply because the leader was afraid of the power the assistant had in the district, sometimes relegating them to lesser roles and stripping them of power or voice in important matters. I believe this is a mistake. Any savvy school administrator should want this administrative assistant to be a major part of the leadership team and thus a powerful ally in spreading positive energy throughout the school.

7. Help leaders set up interviews when necessary and think of every touchpoint for potential employees. Help leadership make a positive first impression—things like preparing what they'll need for the interview, making sure they have a drink, providing comfortable seating, adjusting the thermostat to a comfortable temperature, and checking signage to get to the interview room, to name a few. As a side note, if you are treated rudely by the interviewee, make sure you tell the school leader. If they're not respectful to the office staff, they're not the type of person you or your leader will want in your school.

8. Be another set of eyes for the school leaders. You are aware of so many details about the school that may need leaders' attention, like outdated or incorrect information on the school website/social media pages, grass that needs to be cut or weeds pulled, flags worn or tattered, the marquee outdated, and so on. Having these problems reflects poorly

on the school as a whole. You can own the school by looking for issues like these and reporting them to leadership. This cuts down on complaint calls you'll get from parents and the community and avoids making you, the leader, and the school look bad.

9. Be on the lookout for any social snafus your leaders may encounter. Having a close enough relationship to be able to point out toilet paper sticking to their shoe, food in their teeth, or a stain on their clothing is a great way to give customer service to leadership.

Susan Says: "Mr. Middleton would come in wearing this atrocious coat one year. I dubbed it The Coat of Many Colors. People were talking! I just couldn't let him keep wearing it without saying something. So I told him, 'Mr. Middleton, what in the world are you wearing? You're better off burning it!' He appreciated the advice and stopped wearing the coat. For years afterward, he'd come in wearing that coat as a joke just to get a laugh out of me. When Mr. Middleton called me for a story for this book, I just had to ask him how The Coat of Many Colors was holding up after twenty years."
– Susan Hensley, Administrative Assistant to the Superintendent, Mason County School District

Be a Team with Leadership

As a school leader, I needed front office professionals who were another set of eyes for me, who could think like me, who could be on call 24/7, and who wanted my school, my district, and me to be successful. I was looking for "foxhole" individuals—people I could trust with very important information, to lead the front office, keep me informed, and help me lead the entire school district.

In a normal school setting, leaders make enemies without even trying or knowing. It might just be a school board member with an ax to grind with the superintendent or any of their leaders. It could be a mad parent with social status who drives around the campus and just looks for something to complain about. I need more eyes and ears than just my own. Calls to superiors or to leaders about tattered flags, grass not being cut, filthy restrooms at the ballpark, outdated marquees, buses not following rules, and so on are quite common. Leaders need all hands on deck with school office staff to help them see these issues and have their backs. This type of partnership can at least cut down on the number of complaints and thus give school leadership more time to spend on teaching and learning.

Communication Is Key

I remember having an administrative assistant who would roll her eyes when she did not agree with something the school administration was doing. It was her subtle way of letting our staff know she and I were not in agreement on what was occurring within the school. We both felt the tension growing and, being a new assistant principal, I wasn't sure what to do. She ended up taking the lead and coming to talk to me one-on-one to work this out. Since she had worked with several other administrators, she knew that having a close working relationship was essential to the school. From then on, we worked together on improving communication to salvage our relationship. Putting the work in paid off, as we were on the same page moving forward and stayed good friends until her passing last year. I owe a lot to Mrs. Connie Reffett as she taught this brash young leader many necessary skills that I utilized throughout my career.

9. Relationships with Parents, Families, and the Community

1. Walk parents to their destination when they are lost in order to build a relationship. If you can't do that, have a recruit and train a student. Your goal should be to never let a parent find their destination on their own. You never want a guest to be lost in your school without a school person in their presence. Remember to learn the parent's name and use it when talking with them. We all love to hear our names!

> **Customer Service Stat: "Employees only ask for the customer's name 21% of the time. The person has a name 100% of the time, and they like hearing it." —ContactPoint Client Research**[xiv]

2. When parents come to you with problems about the school, take that opportunity to show empathy to their situation, especially if you can relate. If you've had children in school, you can relay a story about your own kids. For example, if a parent is complaining about their child getting lice at school, if your child has had lice, you can recall what a headache it was for you and your child, showing that you have been in their shoes. Remember to keep the focus on the customer, not on yourself, so use these opportunities as a way to connect, not just to tell your story. Sometimes parents are a little embarrassed about situations that involve their children. It helps them to know that others experience the same issues. *Your goal should be preventing a guest from having the perception of being judged.*

3. Know your visitors. Call them by their names, learn a little about them, and make a connection. This is a great way to find common ground. When a parent calls, tell them you know their child from drama, cheerleading team, math club, or whatever activity they do. Sharing your knowledge of the student can instantly defuse angry parents or tense situations. (This tip works for students as well.) Solving problems in this way makes you invaluable to administrators and makes you the go-to person guests will call and ask for specifically. Think about a doctor's office where you know one receptionist and there's a revolving door of staff. That person you know will not only be able to help you more efficiently (since they know your history) but will also care more about giving you great service because you already have a relationship.

4. Remember that parents and students are always watching your behavior even when you are not working. I've seen office professionals who got caught stealing in public or broke rules and laws and the parents/family found out about it. Acting inappropriately gives you and your school a bad reputation. This is a high-profile position and not one for those who get in trouble or act controversially in their personal time. Getting drunk and being thrown out of a bar is certainly not going to reflect well on the school, but even being rowdy and having to stumble home or call a cab to get home can be seen unfavorably by the community.

5. If we must make someone wait, tell them why, apologize, and see if there is an alternative. For example, if a parent comes in to talk to a teacher, that teacher may not be available at that moment. You can look at their schedule and see when they have a free period or planning period. Check with the teacher to make sure they are available to meet with the parent at that time. Then tell the parent to come back at that time or ask if they'd like to wait. For some, waiting will be the best option. Can you offer them coffee or a snack from the cafeteria while they wait? Try to make their wait as pleasant as possible. Maybe let them sit in the library or another quiet office to give them a more peaceful place to sit than the chaotic main office. If they choose waiting in the office with you, check on them periodically, ask if you can get them anything, or make small talk. We all hate having to sit on an airplane with no information about taking off and indefinitely waiting for the plane to move. Don't re-create that experience for parents in your office!

6. When someone comes in to talk to one of the school staff, you can save a lot of time by educating people about the chain of command. For example, if someone comes in to talk to the principal, you can dig a little bit to see if you could help that person yourself, thus saving everyone's time. If a visitor has an issue with a teacher, you can explain that the principal would ask them if they'd talked to the teacher already, so to save everyone's time, they should talk to the teacher first. Pointing people to the right staff member, especially when they're asking for the wrong person, will save everyone the headache of running around.

7. Take notes when people are talking to help you remember what they say. This also shows the person you are listening to them. You may tell the person on the phone you are taking notes or ask them to speak a little more slowly in order to make sure you get everything correct.

8. Speak with anyone within five feet of you. The best hotels make sure their staff are all saying hello or asking if the guests are enjoying their stay whenever they are near guests. This creates a friendly, welcoming environment and makes people feel like their presence is important.

9. Try to make a good first impression! Research is very clear that people form an impression of you within seconds of first meeting you. You only have one chance to make a good first impression and I've found that it is difficult to change a negative first impression. It can help to think about it like going on a first date.

Office Professionals Are the Face of the Company

This concept played out early in my educational administration years when I became principal of a middle school in central Kentucky. I spoke to a parent who was enrolling her youngest child. She told me she had a son who had attended my middle school a few years earlier and that she hated the school. I pressed this parent on why she had such strong feelings about the school I was about to lead. Did her son fail a grade, did he have terrible test scores, a slew of bad teachers? My mind raced with possibilities as I awaited her answer. She then told me she hated the *receptionist*, who she recalled being very rude to her each time she had called the school. This initial meeting with this parent would help shape my customer service philosophy that is now so ingrained within me to this day. People will base how they feel about the school, leaders, and even the quality of the education on their interactions with just one person. Chances are a school office professional will be that first impression.

10. Through personal experiences, practice finding ways to connect with all customers. It can be something as simple as seeing a customer come into the office wearing a sports team's shirt and asking about that team. I find it helps to ask people where they're from so you can talk about a time you have been to their hometown, or if you haven't, say you've always wanted to go there. If you're still stuck finding a way to connect, it's always a good idea to talk about their child. For visitors or callers who you're expecting, especially when your leader is part of the conversation, do a little research on them or their student first and let your leader know any important information. Practicing this tip can be a lot of work, but it truly does pay off and it separates the average front office professionals from the great ones.

11. Whenever possible, avoid letting long lines of customers form in the main office. Sometimes, this is unavoidable, so do not let people feel they are a ghost and cannot be seen. Try to acknowledge parents and guardians immediately. Let them know you will be right with them.

> "We see our customers as invited guests to a party, and we are the hosts. It's our job every day to make every important aspect of the customer experience a little bit better." —Jeff Bezos[xv]

12. Have a plan for when there is a customer with a complex issue or multiple issues so you can hand them off to someone else and keep the line moving. Having another person available who can tag in once in a while for a customer who needs extra attention will make the customer feel like they are not rushed along to keep the line moving and it will allow you to get to the remaining customers in line in a timely manner. Just be sure to say something like, "Let me get someone who can better serve you," to show you are not simply passing the buck with a problem customer. It's a win for that person and it will be appreciated by those in line behind them.

13. When there is a line of people, show poise. If there is a line and the next person due up is not paying attention—perhaps they're on their cell phone or talking with others—do not yell or become frustrated. Do not just yell "Next!" Practice other methods of getting attention. Try holding up your hand so someone in line might nudge the next person. Maybe say, "Can I help the next person?" in a nice tone. If this problem occurs frequently, you can hand out numbers, like at a deli, so you can just call the next number. And if they don't respond after calling their number a few times, you can move on to the next number.

14. Avoid saying "no" to a parent or guardian without telling them some things you can do for them. Customer service is about giving something, not rationalizing why you are *not* doing something. Look for ways to turn your "no" into a "yes." For example, what if a parent calls to say they'll be late for pickup and the student will need to have an unauthorized person pick them up? Since there's just no way to confirm that the person you're speaking to is the parent, you can't let that unauthorized person pick up the student. Instead of shooting down this idea, you can tell them a staff member will watch the student at the school until the parent can come in.

Also, for any issue where policy doesn't seem to fit the situation, and you think your school leader would want to do something other than the letter of the law, be sure to bring the issue to them. For example, we had a rule that any student who was on in-school suspension cannot participate in after-school activities. A parent calls you with a complaint about the cheerleading team missing their once-a-year competition because one of the cheerleaders was given in-school suspension for that day. Punishing the whole team for one student's behavior isn't in the spirit of the ISS rule, so you bring the issue to the principal, asking if the student's ISS can be moved to the following day, thus allowing the entire team to compete.

Another example is an honor roll student who has had perfect attendance for eight years. The parent calls you, saying her child takes pride in her record but has to leave school right before lunch because of a death in the family. The policy says that if a student leaves after lunch, that student will be given credit for a full day's attendance that day. Find a way to help the student keep her perfect attendance record. Maybe bring the issue to the principal and recommend switching the student's lunch period to an earlier one for just that day.

When the issue simply cannot be turned into a "yes," you can provide empathy. Let's say a student cannot attend a dance because of a school rule that doesn't let them go to events if they have more than two unexcused absences. Instead of saying no and simply citing policy, you can show empathy for them by saying how hard it must be to miss the dance, but there will be another one coming up in the spring. That way, you've kept to the rule, but given them hope by highlighting something they can look forward to in the future.

15. Find the answer—even if it has nothing to do with public education or a customer's student. *As a school office professional, you should know where to find any answer.* If you can't solve the problem yourself, there is a good chance you know someone in the community who can find the answer. Of course, as a last resort, you can usually just google it! The phrase "I'll call and find out for you" should be in the front of your mind at all times when talking with customers. You can't predict the weather, but you can answer questions like, "What time is the elementary school graduation?" Or "What time does Walmart close?"

16. Eliminate certain words and phrases. Try not to say, "It's our policy," "I just can't do this," or "I will not do that." "I am sorry" is another phrase customers hate to hear. Instead, try to use words and phrases like "Yes," "My pleasure," "Can," and "Will." Even using phrases like "We can agree on this . . ." Similar to turning the "no" into a "yes," this tip is a way to focus on what you *can* do for the customer.

17. Always give parents and families information as soon as possible. Make sure your school contacts them directly when there is a change in plans that may affect them such as school supplies, athletic event times, and bus schedules. Do the same for staff, as they are also your customers. For example, if you have to lock the school down because of something happening in the community, you can use the OneCall system to tell parents and families that the lockdown is not about something happening at the school. Or, if there's a recall on orange juice from certain parts of Florida and your school serves orange juice from that state, people may be worried. You can nip this problem in the bud by speaking to the food service director and principal and then alerting families that you've looked into the problem and confirmed that your orange juice is sourced from an unaffected location. You may also want to remind all cocurricular and extracurricular staff to inform the office staff of any change in an activity's schedule, so you have the correct information when confused parents inevitably call the school.

18. If parents bring young children into the school office, give them attention and treat them as future customers. Ask their names, brag on them or something they are wearing, or complement their haircut. This will make a great first impression that may last until they get to school age. It also will make the parent feel better about the school as a whole.

10. Nonverbal Communication and Body Language

1. Smile at everyone (students, staff, parents, vendors, etc.) during every interaction, including phone calls, as everyone can hear the smile in your voice.

2. Be consistent with your mood. Being a school office professional, you really can't have a bad day. It's important to answer the phone with a smile in your voice every time. If you're scheduled to have surgery, would you want to see that the surgeon is having a bad day? Think about a server at a restaurant. Who wants to be served by someone who has a bad attitude or who tries to tell the customer about his or her bad day? The same rules apply for school office staff.

> Research on tone of voice when meeting with people face-to-face indicates that body language and tone account for 93% of communication, while words spoken account for only 7%.[xvi]

3. Be conscious of your body language. Customer service research tells us that 55% of our communication is attributed to body language.[xvii]

- Be cognizant of your arms being crossed.

- Do you sit far away from customers or are you close to the customer?

- Is there a barrier like a table or stand between you and the customer? Are you sitting up higher and looking down on the customer?

- Make a list of traits that you find annoying in others. Self-reflect if you make any of the same mistakes. For example, one of my pet peeves is when people overuse adverbs. How about a person's tone of voice?

"Is It Okay If I Have a Bad Day?"

I have been asked this question many times during my presentations and have heard this excuse from some of my employees through the years. We all wake up on the wrong side of the bed sometimes, but it's crucial for school office staff to put on a professional face when they're at work.

Consider the following quotes and research to see just how important it is to never show a crack in your "office professional face."

"Every contact we have with a customer influences whether or not they'll come back. We have to be great every time or we'll lose them." —Kevin Stirtz, Author of *More Loyal Customers*

A survey of 15,000 consumers found that "1 in 3 customers will leave a brand they love after just one bad experience, while 92% would completely abandon a company after two or three negative interactions." —Super Office, Customer Service Company[xviii]

"News of bad customer service reaches twice as many ears as news of good customer service" —White House Office of Consumer Affairs[xix]

"On average, satisfied customers tell 5 people about good service they receive. Dissatisfied customers tell 10 people about bad service received." —Hal Mather, Author of *Competitive Manufacturing*

For every unsatisfied customer who complains, there are 26% other unhappy customers who say nothing. And of those 26%, 24% won't come back. —U.S. Office of Consumer Affairs[xx]

"81% of companies with strong capabilities and competencies for delivering customer excellence are outperforming their competition." —Peppers & Rogers Group, Customer Experience Maturity Monitor[xxi]

Fact: Even if you achieve 95% customer satisfaction, you still have fifty customers out of every one thousand walking away dissatisfied.

11. Best Practices

1. Own the problem. Treat each customer's situation like it needs a satisfactory solution from you. Use common sense and empathy to drive your decisions to work within what your leadership will allow.

2. Be in the moment when speaking to customers. At the checkout at Kroger, the clerks give full attention to the person during the entire process. In a school office, your attention is constantly being pulled in different directions. Have a plan for how to handle distractions and remember to take care of one thing at a time.

3. Train yourself to look each person in the eye when they are in front of you. Steady eye contact lets them know you are interested in what they are saying and that you are there to help them.

4. Find a way to wow your customers by giving a little bit extra. If a customer comes in and asks where the gymnasium is, walk them there instead of just giving directions. When a guest comes in and needs to wait for someone, offer coffee or water. If a student gets hurt, call to check in with them at the hospital and be sure to alert leadership. One administrative assistant in our elementary school noticed a boy did not have a winter coat. She had a coat she was planning to donate, so she offered it to the boy's family. They accepted and were so grateful for the offer. These little unexpected things make people feel important and show you are committed to giving great customer service. Be creative! There are endless ways to go above and beyond to give a little bit extra.

Sometimes crises will require you to put in a longer school day. It was the last day of school and we received a call from a parent that their child did not get off the bus. The bus driver assured us the child was dropped off at the apartment complex but could not recall if a parent was there to get them as it was a large group drop-off. One of the front office staff rode with me to the apartment complex, and we went door-to-door until we found the child, who had gone home with a neighbor. From the time we received the call, it took about an hour and a half of her time beyond her work hours. As a leader, I never forgot her performance during this emergency!

5. Keep up with emerging technology trends and welcome new challenges. You don't need to jump on every new idea but be open to the possibility of progress. We all get stuck in our ways sometimes, so it's important to keep an open mind and adapt in order to keep up with the competition and give great customer service. For example, I once had an administrative assistant who did not use computers. The demands of the job made it harder and harder for her to get the work done efficiently. Another office employee did not use financial software but a pencil and paper to keep track of finances. While this method worked for her, it ate up valuable time.

6. Keep handouts or a list of important addresses in the area to give to parents who continue to ask for directions each year. They may be asking how to get to other schools in the district, sports fields, places in town (if they're new to the area), or any other popular destination. Each time someone asks for directions, make up a sheet and store it in a file cabinet with a few duplicates. If people don't need written directions, they can type the address into their GPS or phone and you don't have to worry about looking up addresses every time. This is especially important for students and parents who are new to the area and need to learn about resources like cable companies, water services, heating services, and so on. Offer this information when they come in the first time. Parents will really appreciate you going the extra mile for them and will be impressed with your preparedness.

7. Learn and use the concept of "under-promise and over-deliver" for staff, students, parents, and your boss. Almost every time you interact with people, this concept should be influencing your actions and decisions. An example of under-promise/over-deliver would be telling someone you'll get back to them in a couple of days even though you know you'll be able to get back to them within twenty-four hours. In other words, whatever deadline you give people should be *later* than the latest time you know you can make. When you go to a restaurant, you're excited when your table is ready before the estimated wait time is up and annoyed when the wait is longer than they told you. I had a parent come in upset with the school because their student was being picked on in class and the parent was told no one at the school was doing anything about it. One of the front office staff offered to go down and diffuse the situation and told the parent they could talk with me the next day to discuss what we would do about the bullying. She ended up taking a whole hour out of her day to talk with the parent and actually resolved the issue

herself by putting a plan in place. By promising to just diffuse the situation so I could handle it later and then going ahead and taking care of it right then and there, she was practicing under-promise/over-deliver. Doing things like this will make you an invaluable resource to your school, coworkers, and leaders.

> **Time Is of the Essence!**
> "The handful of companies that respond promptly and accurately to customer emails increase trust in their brand, bolster customer satisfaction, and boost sales both online and offline." —BenchmarkPortal[xxii]

8. Always give yourself some wiggle room with your promises to customers. When a parent calls and asks what time the bus will arrive to pick up their student, avoid giving an exact time and instead give a window so they're not disappointed at having to wait or they don't get there in time if the bus is early. Avoid phrases like "I'll get right back to you," as that can mean different things for different people and can set them up to be disappointed.

9. Always let your customers know what you did for them. At Southwest Airlines, they spend a lot of money on commercials to proclaim, "Bags Fly Free." Many times, in education, we forget to sell ourselves. You do a lot of work that does not get noticed or appreciated, so sometimes it's important to let people know just how much you do. They're often impressed! When taking care of several issues for a customer, repeat back what you did for them. For example, when you're enrolling a new student who is anxious about their first day and the parent calls looking for reassurance, say, "We talked to all your student's teachers, checked her schedules, made sure there is plenty of time for her to eat, figured out her bus assignment, and spoke with the volleyball coach to let him know your student wants to join the team." Listing what you've done back to the customer reassures them that you're on top of it and they're in good hands.

The Amazing School Office Professional: "The School Secretary runs the whole school. You have to see her for everything! She's got radar, sonar and kid-ar. She'll just string you up with two of her eight arms, while the other six are sending emails, sorting letters, stacking forms, signing slips, sticking on bandages, and scheduling conferences. She must spend a fortune on underarm deodorant!" —*The School Secretary from the Black Lagoon* by Mike Thaler[xxiii]

10. Don't engage in negativity from families, the community, or staff. Consider this scenario: A school disciplines a student, and the parent calls and asks you if they can talk to the principal. The parent then says to you, "The principal treats my child so badly at this school." At this point, you have a choice. You can agree—"Yes, sometimes he has bad days"; disagree—"I've watched him handle students and nobody handles them better than he does"; or stick with the task at hand—"I'm sorry you feel that way. I'll make sure he gets that message." Staying neutral and not picking sides when someone vents to you about someone else will allow you to focus on your work and not get sucked into the drama. Change the subject or ask if you'd like them to leave a message for the person they're talking about.

11. Play music whenever possible. Having music on in your office or anywhere at the school can be a positive mood boost for students, staff, and guests. Do you have a favorite holiday music playlist? What about going old school playing albums on a record player to teach students how it used to be back in the day? Some schools will play a school song over the intercom at the beginning of each school day ("We Are Family") or to celebrate a win ("We Are the Champions"). How about playing songs from the upcoming school musical to get everyone excited for the production?

12. Own your school. Show initiative beyond the job description. Go above and beyond the call of duty for the sake of making the school, leadership, and your department look good.

Closing

I hope this book has been useful to you. If just one tip helps you or your school/district, teacher, or student in the area of customer service and public relations, it fulfills my mission for writing it. I would advise that you read and reflect on these tips three to five at a time. Due to the variety of school office professional positions, each tip may be applied to each person differently and some may not apply at all. I took a lot of time asking questions and discussing parts of this book with some of the best office professionals I have come across in my thirty-two years in public education. I also spoke with several leaders about topics from this book and I can say that, without exception, all reenforced the importance of school office professionals to school districts, staff, students, and community.

By reading this book, it should be evident I hold these positions and the people in these positions in the highest regard. Thank you for what you do each and every day in the public school system. You are on the front lines and down in the trenches with school staff, leaders, parents, and community. As all the various types of school choice continues to grow, along with competition for students, so, too, will the importance of your positions. In my opinion, you are truly the gatekeepers for your school and an integral part in the success and future of public education.

Other Books by Kelly E. Middleton

- *Who Cares? Improving Public Schools Through Relationships and Customer Service* (2007)

- *Simply the Best: 29 Things Students Say the Best Teachers Do Around Relationships* (2010)

- *Competing for Kids: 21 Customer Service Concepts Public Schools Can Use to Retain and Attract Students* (2018)

- *Feed Our Students Well: 18 Customer Service Concepts for Public School Food Service* (2020)

www.kellymiddleton.com

Endnotes

i Help Scout, *75 Customer Service Facts, Quotes and Statistics: How Your Business Can Deliver with the Best of the Best*. Retrieved from helpscout.net.

ii "20 Great Customer Service Quotes," Customer Thermometer. Accessed June 2, 2021, https://www.customerthermometer.com/customer-experience/20-great-customer-experience-quotes/.

iii Fink, Harry Julian, and R.M. Fink, *Big Jake*, directed by George Sherman (1971; Los Angeles: Batjak Productions, Film).

iv "Service Is Key," The DQ Week. Accessed June 3, 2021, https://www.dqweek.com/service-is-the-key/.

v "Ultimate Guide to Customer Service Channels," Chatra. Accessed June 3, 2021, https://chatra.com/books/ultimate-guide-to-customer-service-channels/04-email-support/#:~:text=Forrester%20Research%20found%20that%2041,14%25%20never%20respond%20at%20all.&text=Pew%20Research%20discovered%2092%25%20of,it%20on%20an%20average%20day.

vi "Consumer Reports Most Irritating Customer Service Pain Points August 2015," Marking Charts. Accessed June 3, 2021, https://www.marketingcharts.com/charts/consumerreports-most-irritating-customer-service-pain-points-aug2015.

vii "8 Key Points of Great Customer Service Revealed Through Inspiring Quotes," HelpCenter. Accessed June 3, 2021, https://www.helpcenterapp.com/blog/8-key-points-of-great-customer-service-revealed-through-inspiring-quotes/.

viii Denove, Chris, and James D. Power IV, *Satisfaction: How Every Great Company Listens to the Voice of the Customer*. New York: Portfolio, 2006. Print.

ix Blanchard, Ken, and Margaret McBride, *The One Minute Apology: A Powerful Way to Make Things Better*. New York: William Morrow, 2003. Print.

x End User Feedback (@EndUserFeedback). 2017. "27% Of Email Inquiries Sent to Online Retailers Are Answered Incorrectly. #CustomerService Pic.twitter.com/3tFecnOHyL," Twitter, November 27, 2017, 8:00pm. www.twitter.com/EndUserFeedback/status/935312395517313025.

xi Cary, Donnick, "Tiny Problems," *A.P. Bio*, season 3, episode 1, directed by Oz Rodriguez, aired September 3, 2020 (Los Angeles: Peacock, 2020). Television.

xii Weil, Simone, *Gravity and Grace*. New York: Routledge, 1947. Print.

xiii Newell-Legner, Ruby, "Leader's Guide: Secrets to Keeping Our Customers Happy!" RubySpeaks Inc., 2008.

xiv Help Scout, *75 Customer Service Facts, Quotes and Statistics: How Your Business Can Deliver with the Best of the Best*. Retrieved from helpscout.net.

xv Greathouse, John, "5 Time-Tested Success Tips from Amazon Founder Jeff Bezos," *Forbes*, April 13, 2013. https://www.forbes.com/sites/johngreathouse/2013/04/30/5-time-tested-success-tips-from-amazon-founder-jeff-bezos/?sh=314c8f57370c.

xvi Belludi, Nagesh, "Albert Mehrabian's 7-38-55 Rule of Personal Communication," *Right Attitudes*, October 8, 2008. https://www.rightattitudes.com/2008/10/04/7-38-55-rule-personal-communication/.

xvii Belludi, Nagesh, "Albert Mehrabian's 7-38-55 Rule of Personal Communication," *Right Attitudes*, October 8, 2008. https://www.rightattitudes.com/2008/10/04/7-38-55-rule-personal-communication/.

xviii Kulbytė, Toma, "37 Customer Experience Statistics You Need to Know for 2021," *Super Office,* May 3, 2021. https://www.superoffice.com/blog/customer-experience-statistics/

xix Clapp, Randy, "What Is the True Cost of Losing a Customer?" *Advantage Communications*, April 9, 2019. https://www.advantagecall.com/blog/what-is-the-true-cost-of-losing-a-customer.

xx Jacobs, Daniel G., "Walk the Talk," *Smart Business*, July 22, 2002. http://www.sbnonline.com/article/walk-the-talk-tips-for-the-company-in-need-of-customer-service-help/.

xxi *Customer Experience Maturity Monitor*. SAS Institute Inc., Jubelirer Research and Peppers & Rogers Group. 2009. https://na.eventscloud.com/file_uploads/27f707356d2d1aa82e1cf826544781ff_SAS_Customer_Experience_Maturity_Monitor.pdf.

xxii Help Scout, *75 Customer Service Facts, Quotes and Statistics: How Your Business Can Deliver with the Best of the Best*. Retrieved from helpscout.net.

xxiii Thaler, Mike, *The School Secretary from the Black Lagoon* (New York: Scholastic, January 1, 2014). Print.

www.ingramcontent.com/pod-product-compliance
Lightning Source LLC
Chambersburg PA
CBHW041217030426
42336CB00023B/3376